THE BRANDYWINE HERITAGE

ANDREW WYETH   **97**   **British at Brandywine**   1962

THE BRANDYWINE HERITAGE

Howard Pyle   N.C. Wyeth   Andrew Wyeth   James Wyeth

The Brandywine River Museum, Chadds Ford, Pennsylvania

Distributed by New York Graphic Society Ltd., Greenwich, Connecticut

This catalog is dedicated to those remarkable Americans who made it possible through the Brandywine River Museum and its parent organization, the Tri-County Conservancy, to preserve the land and its heritage for future generations.

GEORGE A. WEYMOUTH
President
Tri-County Conservancy

Lenders

MR. and MRS. DOUGLAS ALLEN
Somerville, New Jersey

MR. and MRS. CHARLES M. ALLMOND III
Wilmington, Delaware

LEROY BENGE, SR.
Yorklyn, Delaware

AMANDA BERLS
New York, New York

BOSTON PUBLIC LIBRARY
Boston, Massachusetts

MR. and MRS. J. BRUCE BREDIN
Greenville, Delaware

MR. and MRS. BAIRD C. BRITTINGHAM
Wilmington, Delaware

MR. and MRS. BRIGHAM BRITTON
Cleveland, Ohio

MR. and MRS. HOWARD P. BROKAW
Montchanin, Delaware

THOMAS BROKAW
Montchanin, Delaware

BROWN COUNTY LIBRARY
Green Bay, Wisconsin

MR. and MRS. P. W. TATE BROWN
New York, New York

MR. and MRS. NORMAN L. CAHNERS
Brookline, Massachusetts

MR. and MRS. CARL A. CANTERA
Wilmington, Delaware

CHADDS FORD GALLERY
Chadds Ford, Pennsylvania

FREDERICK C. CHURCH
Boston, Massachusetts

MRS. J. MARSHALL COLE
New Hope, Pennsylvania

MR. and MRS. REED COLEMAN
Madison, Wisconsin

DR. and MRS. NORMAN CRISP
Nashua, New Hampshire

MR. and MRS. BROWNLEE O. CURRY, JR.
New York, New York

STATE OF DELAWARE
OFFICE OF THE ADJUTANT GENERAL
of the State of Delaware

MR. and MRS. DANIEL W. DIETRICH II
Villanova, Pennsylvania

MR. and MRS. EUGENE DIXON
Philadelphia, Pennsylvania

MR. and MRS. RICHARD S. duPONT
Greenville, Delaware

WILLIAM A. FARNSWORTH LIBRARY
AND ART MUSEUM
Rockland, Maine

DR. MARGARET I. HANDY
Chadds Ford, Pennsylvania

MR. and MRS. GORDON HANES
Winston-Salem, North Carolina

THE HON. and MRS. HARRY G. HASKELL, JR.
Wilmington, Delaware

MR. and MRS. H. T. HILLIARD
San Francisco, California

MR. and MRS. DAVID HILYARD
Suffield, Connecticut

FREDERICK L. HOLBORN
Washington, D.C.

MR. and MRS. GEORGE E. KEARNS, JR.
Westtown, Pennsylvania

MR. and MRS. RICHARD V. KING
Chadds Ford, Pennsylvania

MR. and MRS. JOHN S. KISTLER
West Chester, Pennsylvania

MR. and MRS. WALTER J. LAIRD, JR.
Wilmington, Delaware

MR. and MRS. RICHARD C. LAYTON
Wilmington, Delaware

MR. and MRS. JOSEPH E. LEVINE
New York, New York

RICHARD LEVINE
New York, New York

CHESTER MARRON
Ramsey, New Jersey

MR. and MRS. JOHN W. McCOY II
Chadds Ford, Pennsylvania

MR. and MRS. EDWARD McLAUGHLIN
Easton, Connecticut

JAMES P. MILLS, SR.
Middleburg, Virginia

DR. and MRS. WILLIAM A. MORTON
West Chester, Pennsylvania

MRS. WILLIAM E. PHELPS
Montchanin, Delaware

MR. and MRS. CARL D. PRATT
West Chester, Pennsylvania

MR. and MRS. W. GLASGOW REYNOLDS
Greenville, Delaware

MR. and MRS. RICHARD RIEGEL, JR.
Wilmington, Delaware

MR. and MRS. JOHN W. ROLLINS, JR.
Greenville, Delaware

FRANK E. SCHOONOVER
Wilmington, Delaware

CHARLES SCRIBNERS SONS
New York, New York

CHARLES SEAVERNS
Hartford, Connecticut

MR. and MRS. WILLIAM V. SIPPLE
Milford, Delaware

MRS. ANDREW J. SORDONI
Forty-Fort, Pennsylvania

MR. and MRS. GEORGE E. TENER
Middlebury, Virginia

MRS. JAMES THEODORE
Chadds Ford, Pennsylvania

JEFFREY THEODORE
Chadds Ford, Pennsylvania

ALEXANDER F. TREADWELL
New York, New York

MR. and MRS. EDWIN S. TULLIS
New York, New York

J. ROBINSON WEST
Unionville, Pennsylvania

MR. and MRS. GEORGE A. WEYMOUTH
Chadds Ford, Pennsylvania

MR. and MRS. GEORGE T. WEYMOUTH
Greenville, Delaware

WILMINGTON Y.M.C.A.
Wilmington, Delaware

MR. and MRS. ROBERT F. WOOLWORTH
New York, New York

MR. and MRS. ANDREW WYETH
Chadds Ford, Pennsylvania

MR. and MRS. JAMES B. WYETH
Chadds Ford, Pennsylvania

MRS. N.C. WYETH
Chadds Ford, Pennsylvania

MR. and MRS. NATHANIEL C. WYETH
Mendenhall, Delaware

NICHOLAS WYETH
New York, New York

RUTH A. YERION
New York, New York

AND ANONYMOUS LENDERS

Foreword

Considering the traditional American pride in resourcefulness and ingenuity, it is a curious conceit of recent artistic criticism to belittle illustration and illustrators. Even when someone is credited with being a successful illustrator, he is somehow thereby deprived of the elevated status of artist. The fact of the matter is that American artists have traditionally turned their hands to a variety of tasks as practicality or fancy might dictate. The creative mind in America has never been satisfied to follow those neatly defined channels of expression which have characterized much of European art during recent centuries. The American muse is an unruly sort of girl with an entirely feminine and charming tendency toward the unpredictable. When Robert Fulton, for example,— no mean portraitist—, ran out of funds in Paris with which to finance his experiments on the steamboat, he painted a large panorama of *The Burning of Moscow,* advertised it, charged admission, and when he had made enough money, turned back to the steamboat. Samuel F.B. Morse displayed similar versatility. His life-size, full-length *Lafayette* in New York's City Hall is one of the outstanding portraits of the period, and we all know what he did with the telegraph, though I am afraid too few of us know what he achieved with the paint brush. It was the once-famous American neo-classic sculptor, Horatio Greenough, who, around the middle of the last century, first warned us of the willfulness of the American muse when he recognized the developing clipper ship, brought to perfection by Donald McKay, along with the large-wheeled, light-as-a-feather trotting wagon, as works of art. Indeed, he went further and anticipated a new American esthetic which many of us have not yet quite caught up with after more than a century, when he defined beauty as "the promise of function."

To turn specifically to the matter of the artist and the illustrator, our history shows that it would be a denial of the American tradition to separate the two, relegating each to a different level of achievement. Asher B. Durand, one of the leading landscapists of the 19th century, and for years the respected president of the National Academy, was not only a skilled engraver, but also an illustrator. So were George Catlin, Winslow Homer, Elihu Vedder, and Frederic Remington, not to mention several members of The Eight, among them William Glackens and John Sloan. And there are many other examples, major and minor, as well.

The real distinction lies elsewhere, in the illustrator's ability, in Pyle's words, "to fill out the text rather than to make a picture of some scene described in it." As he told his students, it is "the difference between creative and imitative art" that matters. With true American pragmatism, he taught his pupils that when "making pictures to be reproduced in print you are then given no favor and your pictures must be good as pictures or else they are of no possible use." His "final aim in teaching" was to produce "painters of pictures." "To this end," he wrote, "I regard magazine and book illustration as a ground from which to produce painters."

In Pyle's own work, his wide-ranging imagination combined with a hard-won technical versatility enabled him to give convincing form to many characters and episodes of history and fiction. This gift he shared with his most distinguished pupil, N.C. Wyeth. For several generations of Americans, the mention of the pirate Blackbeard, of Robin Hood, of the knights of the round table, of characters from *Treasure Island, Kidnapped,* and *The Black Arrow* brings to mind with vivid clarity the creations of Howard Pyle and N.C. Wyeth. This achievement certainly admits them to the highest echelon of illustrators. And, when one sees the originals of those familiar and compelling illustrations, whether in the knowingly controlled line in black and white, or in the painterly handling of oil, there can remain little doubt about their being genuine artists as well.

Both men were, and to a great extent still are, broadly popular artists, a quality they share with N.C.'s son Andrew and his grandson, James. All are closely identified with the Brandywine valley and Chadds Ford. Pyle had known the area well since boyhood. He lived and taught in Wilmington, though for some years he commuted to Philadelphia, where his classes at the Drexel Institute (1894–1900) won a similar loyalty from his pupils as had those of Thomas Eakins at the Pennsylvania Academy a decade or so earlier. Pyle conducted a summer school at Chadds Ford for some years, and it was there that N.C. Wyeth settled after early years in Needham, outside Boston, and youthful adventures in the still wild West.

The New England connection has been maintained by the Wyeths through summers on the Maine coast. Within a world limited to the valley's gentle slopes, water meadows, and upland fields defined by forests of hardwoods, and the austere northern shore, rocky and windswept, first N.C., and then Andrew, and now James have found all the scope necessary for their art. For all of them, it has been an art unusually self-motivated and self-developed. Pyle's brief study in his teens with a totally unknown, Antwerp-trained artist named Van der Weilen, and a year or so's rather hit-or-miss attendance at the Art Students' League in New York, provided basic academic fundamentals. His anatomical work with a Philadelphia surgeon — a parallel to Eakins' rigorous training — was probably more significant for his future. Beyond this he charted his own course, driven by a powerful determination. As demanding of himself as of his students, he developed within his own work what he sought to bring out in theirs — resolved expressions of a richly pictorial imagination. "Pictures," he wrote to a friend, "are the creations of the imagination and not of technical facility, and that . . . which art students most need is the cultivation of their imagination and its direction into practical and useful channels of creation — and I hold that this is exactly in line with all other kinds of professional education, whether of law, medicine, finance, or physics. I would not belittle the necessity of accurate technical training. I insist upon that in my own school even more strenuously than it is insisted upon in the great art schools of the country; but I subordinate that technical training entirely to the training of the imagination . . ."

N.C. Wyeth had had some formal training in the Massachusetts Normal Art School and the Eric Pape School in Boston. More than any other of Pyle's pupils, he responded to the intense cultivation of the imagination, giving it a robust expression which reflects his boundless energy and outgoing attitude toward life in complete contrast to Pyle's iron reserve. Wyeth, in turn, and in his own distinctive way, passed on the tradition to his son Andrew as well as to his daughters Henriette and Carolyn, and Andrew continued in the training of his son James. So what is represented by this exhibition is a kind of artistic dynasty comparable in American art only to the painting Peales of Philadelphia. Except for Henriette, who married one of her father's pupils, Peter Hurd, landscapist, portrait painter, and artistic interpreter of the mountains and the deserts of the Southwest, the rest have maintained the same close relation with the valley. Yet it has not been as a refuge from reality, but rather as a base, free of suburbia's petty distractions, with an atmosphere sympathetic to the individualistic and creative life.

Because of his introspective nature, perhaps the result of Swedenborgian mysticism superimposed on a Quaker heritage, Howard Pyle lived an intense inner life which enabled him to realize with such completeness imaginative works like his *Robin Hood,* in which literary style, illustration, decoration, and typography are combined to produce a creative whole. On the other hand his practicality enabled him to adjust to the varying developments in reproductive techniques used by the publishers with whom he worked. Like Winslow Homer in his illustrations, Pyle had a sense for the large design which could be translated by the wood engravers with maximum effectiveness and minimum loss in the process. Yet his conscientiousness led him to carry out the originals as works of art in their own right. For example, the original — *The Wreck* — for an illustration for one of his own stories for *Harper's New Monthly Magazine* entitled "Among the Sand Hills," which was to be reproduced smaller than a post card, is a two by three foot canvas painted with breadth and a rich impasto which reveal something of the emotional life of the artist hidden beneath an austere though gentle exterior.

We know from the record that Pyle was aware of what was going on in the art world, both at home and abroad. His own reputation became widespread: Van Gogh mentioned him in a letter to his brother Theo. There is evidence in Pyle's work of his interest in the Pre-Raphaelites, and also, rather surprisingly, of the sinuous forms of l'Art Nouveau perhaps seen in reproductions or through the designs of Louis C. Tiffany, since Pyle did not go abroad until 1910 and died within the year in Italy. His range of imagination led him into some curiously effective works with suggestions of the mysterious and the sinister, and his preoccupation with pirates, whose bloodthirsty proclivities he did little to minimize, has overtones of violence oddly at variance with his outward personality.

He was very fortunate in living during a golden age of illustration, both in book and magazine publishing. The editors of such periodicals as *Appleton's Magazine, Harper's,* and others sought out the best talents, both in writing and illustration, and employed the most expert engravers, whether on wood or metal. This taste and craftsmanship appear in the often delightfully composed pages combining black and white illustration with type. The substitution in 1877 of white-line wood engraving for the previous black-line technique, (both employing the engraver's burin in the end grain of a box-wood block), largely as the result of the demanding standards of Alexander W. Drake, art editor of *Scribner's* in the '70's, and later of its successor, *The Century,* and of

St. Nicholas, enabled the increasingly atmospheric effects sought by the artists to be rendered with greater delicacy. The richer blacks of the black-line technique, by means of which compositions were reproduced by cutting away the block's surface so that the resulting raised areas transferred the ink to the paper, allowed stronger formal definition. But the white-line method, in which the cutter made tiny dots, flecks, and grooves in the block's surface, provided greater nuance and gradation of value. This combination of skill and artistry made the last quarter of the century outstanding in the quality of its publications.

Steel engraving and lithography were also used, the former more freely than the latter because of a lack of trained lithographers. The introduction of mechanical techniques around the turn of the century brought to an end this collaboration of skills. Later, illustrations were merely dropped in, full-page, at convenient intervals. Fortunately for posterity, Pyle wrote and illustrated the greater number of his best works during this fertile period, and turned increasingly to other tasks, including large mural paintings, during his later years. The introduction of the four-color process brought an added dimension into publishing, yet, in general, despite the charms of color, the old graphic unity of the book or magazine was lost.

Pyle's lettering was excellent, and his sense of the combination of lettering and illustration, as on covers and titles, was highly developed. Though N.C. Wyeth must have learned something of this from Pyle, he has his own marked abilities in this field. Yet it was only in a few of his later works that he was free to design complete titles and covers, so mechanical had book-production become. His largeness of spirit and natural enthusiasm led him to paint the originals for illustrations, which were to be reproduced at the scale of the page of a normal-size bound volume, in the form of large canvasses which are unmistakably paintings in their own right. They show his love for the oil medium in their rich and textured surfaces, broadly handled, and painterly far beyond the necessities of illustration. Where Pyle's compositions were often carefully architectural and tended to be linear in structure, Wyeth's seem spontaneous and organic, made up of large forms, curving outlines, and dramatic light and shade with rich color. His characters are more strongly individualized than Pyle's. They have an earthiness and often a touch of robust humor. They are full of life and gusto, and have none of the delicate fantasy which sometimes appears in Pyle. Yet they have invention and variety, and also, in their larger forms and dramatic use of dark shadow often have a touch of the sinister. Their mood is pervasive, their images powerful. Their range is from the brutal effectiveness of *Blind Pew* through the suspenseful, momentary silence of *The Vedette* to the sensitivity of *The Newborn Calf*. Pyle occasionally lapsed into sentiment, Wyeth never.

Pyle was eclectic in a positive, not a negative sense. He was also influenced by Holbein, Hogarth, and the early German masters, especially Dürer, as seen in his command of a decorative line which appears in his *Robin Hood*, Arthurian books, *The Wonder Clock*, and *Otto of the Silver Hand*. Yet it was his own line, controlled by his own sense of order. Wyeth also had a personal line in his black and white work, and a sense of the relation of drawing to the book, but, because of the changes of the times, he had less opportunity to show his individuality in this way. Instead, his distinctive artistic personality, reflecting Emersonian ideals no doubt acquired during his New England boyhood, led him into a more personal involvement with life in his art, resulting in a vividness of impact which was all his own. He lived the precepts which Pyle offered his pupils: "throw your heart into the picture then jump in after it . . .; feel the wind and rain on your skin when you paint it . . ." Because he naturally thought large, Wyeth also did a number of murals. Unfortunately he wrote far less than Pyle, though we know from articles and letters that he had a lively prose style and a feeling for mood and drama parallel to that shown in his painting. Both shared an intense preoccupation with the past, not as something dead and gone, but as made up of living, feeling people. Both accumulated a large collection of ancient costumes, uniforms, and artifacts. Where Pyle was scholarly in every detail of his historical compositions, and was factual to a degree, Wyeth felt them as well as accurately recreated them, and tended to identify the past with his own experience, using familiar sights, models and objects from his own environment in a way which anticipates the approach of his son Andrew.

Early in his career, Andrew Wyeth also did some illustrating. Then came the early water colors, a medium that he made his own. In this he is in the line of Winslow Homer, John Marin, and Charles Burchfield, because only in America has water color been considered and used as a major medium comparable to oil. Later came the temperas, an ancient, exacting medium which imposes its own contemplative pace, learned from Peter Hurd. Andrew's basic training as an artist was while growing up in his father's studio. There, under a kindly but exacting paternal eye, he developed the command of means which Pyle had demanded, and there was never a lack of stimulus for the imagination. Illness, suffering, and the shock of his father's untimely death at a railroad crossing brought greater depth and maturity to his art.

Andrew shares with his father and with Pyle a special sense of time, but in his own way; he does not paint the past, but rather the evidences of it. He also has an intense sense of place as well as of moment, based upon an analytical vision, increasingly selective and often almost microscopic. More often than not without human figures, and almost invariably in a muted, autumnal palette, his pictures almost always show a "trace of man." They have a hushed quiet which frequently implies an imminent transition, the inevitability of change. When figures do occur, they often seem symbolic, of the unfolding awareness of youth, of the dignity of work, and of age. Invariably his pictures, whether large temperas or small dry-brush drawings, are the result of elimination, a rigorous process of abstraction which reduces every composition to its basic elements. They raise, as do the poems of Robert Frost, the colloquial and the regional to the realm of common human experience, though, paradoxically, in the most personal terms.

From Colonial days, life in the New World, with its vastness, impersonality, and variety, tended to encourage two opposing directions of thought and feeling. Because of the smallness of man in the face of limitless, empty horizons, people clung to the factual, the palpable. In painting this tendency reached its most extreme expression in the trompe l'oeil works of William M. Harnett and John F. Peto, whose still lifes become almost a substitute reality. But the same experience drove man in upon himself, to an inward-looking, visionary, and very personal view, as in the paintings of Albert P. Ryder and of the brilliant anatomist, William Rimmer. This dichotomy appears to some extent in Pyle though somewhat less so in the elder Wyeth, but in Andrew's most successful works both tendencies are combined and reconciled. Objective reality becomes a point of departure for a personal yet sharable inner experience, in which communication exists at both an intellectual and an emotional or instinctive level — a richness of allusion with a minimum of means, Emerson's "the meal in a firkin; the milk in a pan . . ."

Despite the apparently sequestered life spent between Philadelphia, Wilmington, and the valley in the case of Pyle, and Maine and Chadds Ford in the case of the Wyeths, they all share certain qualities and attitudes which often reappear in various expressions of the American creative mind. I have mentioned the suggestion of the sinister in Pyle's and N.C. Wyeth's paintings. It becomes more of an elegiac mood in Andrew's work, yet in its various forms it represents that "power of blackness" that Hawthorne saw as a common thread running through American life and experience. All show a special preoccupation with the sea as a symbol of elemental force, Whitman's "cradle endlessly rocking," a real protagonist in the greatest of American prose works, Melville's *Moby Dick*. All stand in a definite relation to the broad spectrum of American art, from the subjective to the objective. All tend somewhat to look inward as well as outward, though none as strongly as Andrew. A personal relation with nature, part fact and part symbol, runs through their work. There is an American extravagance in the intensity of their vision. Their sense of time's passing reflects the feeling of life as a passage, or as a voyage, as in Ryder's sea pieces and in the most famous series of paintings in American art, Thomas Cole's *Voyage of Life*.

There is a Thoreau-like sense of place in Andrew's work which appears in less definite form in his father's and Pyle's landscapes. He also expresses a feeling of aloneness, of the solitariness of man in contrast to the impersonal grandeur of nature, the essential subject which rose to epic scale in Winslow Homer's mature work. There is an individualism related to that to which Eakins gave most powerful expression, along with a recurring echo of melancholy, related to the feeling of time's passage, which often shadows the American imagination. Most basically, there is great seriousness and dedication, not to the exclusion of joy in life, in nature, and in experience, but as an undercurrent which is the single most important element to creative expression.

In the work of Andrew and his father, Pyle's faith in illustration as "a ground to produce painters" has proven justified. Andrew's son James, thanks to his father's instruction and direction and to his own application, has more than adequately shown his command of that technical facility which Pyle took for granted as a necessary means. The brilliance of his precocious achievement gives promise that Pyle's belief will prove true in another generation as well, as he finds his own distinctive voice, strengthened by a distillation of experience, and fully realizes the potential he seeks. It is good to know that the tradition continues.

Richard McLanathan

New York
April, 1971

Howard Pyle

1 A Verse with A Moral, but No Name (*Pepper and Salt* by Howard Pyle) Harper and Brothers, 1885
Medium: Pen & ink
Size: 15 x 10½ inches
Lender: Anonymous

2 "I Am Captain John Mackra" Said I, and Sat Down Upon the Gunwale of the Boat (*The Rose of Paradise* by Howard Pyle) Harper and Brothers, 1888
Medium: Sepia wash
Size: 10 x 16 inches
Lender: Anonymous

3 Morgan at Porto Bello (*Morgan* by E. C. Stedman) Harpers New Monthly Magazine, December 1888
Medium: Oil
Size: 15 x 24 inches
Lender: Mr. and Mrs. Douglas Allen

4 Decorative Initial (*Jamaica, New and Old* by Howard Pyle) Harpers New Monthly Magazine, January 1890
Medium: Blue wash
Size: 6½ x 2½ inches
Lender: Anonymous

5 Gallows Point (*Jamaica, New and Old* by Howard Pyle) Harpers New Monthly Magazine, January 1890
Medium: Blue wash
Size: 6½ x 2¾ inches
Lender: Anonymous

6 Catch A Gleam from Her Wicked Eye
(*The Broomstick Train* by Oliver Wendell Holmes) Houghton Mifflin Company, 1892
Medium: Pen & ink
Size: 6½ x 4½ inches
Lender: Mr. Andrew Wyeth

7 The Little Maid at The Door (*The Little Maid at the Door* by Mary E. Wilkins) Harpers New Monthly Magazine, February 1892
Medium: Oil on canvas
Size: 16½ x 11¼ inches
Lender: Mr. and Mrs. Charles Allmond III

8 The Wreck (*Among the Sand Hills* by Howard Pyle) Harpers New Monthly Magazine, September 1892
Medium: Oil on canvas
Size: 24 x 36 inches
Lender: Anonymous

9 Along The Canal in Old Manhattan (*The Evolution of New York* by Thomas A. Janvier) Harpers New Monthly Magazine, May 1893
Medium: Oil on illustration board
Size: 18 x 11½ inches
Lender: Anonymous

10 British Fleet in Charlestown Harbor
(*Grandmother's Story of Bunker Hill Battle,* Vol. XIII, works by Oliver Wendell Holmes)
Houghton Mifflin Company, 1893
Medium: Pen & ink
Size: 6 x 3¾ inches
Lender: Mr. and Mrs. Douglas Allen

11 Viewing the Battle (*Grandmother's Story of Bunker Hill Battle,* Vol. XIII, works by Oliver Wendell Holmes) Houghton Mifflin Company, 1893
Medium: Pen & ink
Size 6¼ x 4 inches
Lender: Mr. and Mrs. Richard Layton

12 He Found the Captain Agreeable and Companionable (*Sea Robbers of New York* by Thomas A. Janvier) Harpers New Monthly Magazine, November 1894
Medium: Black-and-white oil on illustration board
Size: 16 x 10½ inches
Lender: Anonymous

13 Mr. Parker Stood Looking Steadily at His Visitor
(Blackbeard) (*Jack Ballister's Fortunes* by Howard Pyle) Century Company, 1895
Medium: Oil on canvas
Size: 10½ x 16 inches
Lender: Mr. Andrew Wyeth

14 The Pirates Fire Upon the Fugitives (*Jack Ballister's Fortunes* by Howard Pyle) Century Company, 1895
Medium: Oil on illustration board
Size: 16 x 10½ inches
Lender: Anonymous

15 Floating Neighbors (*Through Inland Waters* by Howard Pyle) Harpers New Monthly Magazine, 1896
Medium: Oil on illustration board
Size: 11¾ x 9¼ inches
Lender: Anonymous

16 Through Peaceful Stretches (*Through Inland Waters* by Howard Pyle) Harpers New Monthly Magazine, 1896
Medium: Oil on illustration board
Size: 6¾ x 12¼ inches
Lender: Anonymous

17 The Mizzen Top of The Redoubtable (*Nelson at Trafalgar* by A. T. Mahan) Century Magazine, March 1897
Medium: Oil on canvas
Size: 28 x 18 inches
Lender: Anonymous

18 Nelson Sealing His Letter to The Crown Prince of Denmark (*The Battle of Copenhagen* by A. T. Mahan) Century Magazine, March 1897
Medium: Oil on canvas
Size: 16 x 25 inches
Lender: Anonymous

19 Burial of Braddock (*George Washington* by Woodrow Wilson) Harper and Brothers, 1898
Medium: Oil on illustration board
Size: 17⅞ x 11¾ inches
Lender: Boston Public Library

20 In the Old Raleigh Tavern (*George Washington* by Woodrow Wilson. Harper and Brothers, 1898
Medium: Oil on illustration board
Size: 17¾ x 11⅝ inches
Lender: Boston Public Library

21 Leaving Mount Vernon for the Congress of the Colonies (*George Washington* by Woodrow Wilson) Harper and Brothers, 1898
Medium: Oil on illustration board
Size: 17¾ x 11¾ inches
Lender: Boston Public Library

22 A Virginia Plantation Wharf (*George Washington* by Woodrow Wilson) Harper and Brothers, 1898
Medium: Oil on illustration board
Size: 17¾ x 11¾ inches
Lender: Boston Public Library

23 A Virginia Planter (*George Washington* by Woodrow Wilson) Harper and Brothers, 1898
Medium: Oil on illustration board
Size: 24¼ x 15¼ inches
Lender: Boston Public Library

24 Washington and Mary Philipse (*George Washington* by Woodrow Wilson) Harper and Brothers, 1898
Medium: Oil on illustration board
Size: 24¼ x 15¼ inches
Lender: Boston Public Library

25 Washington and von Steuben at Valley Forge (*George Washington* by Woodrow Wilson)
Harper and Brothers, 1898
Medium: Oil on illustration board
Size: 17½ x 11¾ inches
Lender: Boston Public Library

26 Death of Washington (*George Washington* by Woodrow Wilson) Harper and Brothers, 1898
Medium: Oil on illustration board
Size: 21⅞ x 14¾ inches
Lender: Boston Public Library

27 Arrival of Stuyvesant in New Amsterdam (*Colonies and Nation* by Woodrow Wilson)
Harpers Monthly Magazine, February 1901
Medium: Black-and-white oil
Size: 24 x 18 inches
Lender: Brown County Library

28 The Capitulation of Louisberg (*Colonies and Nation* by Woodrow Wilson) Harpers Monthly Magazine, June 1901
Medium: Black-and-white oil
Size: 24 x 18 inches
Lender: Brown County Library

29 A Political Discussion (*Colonies and Nation* by Woodrow Wilson) Harpers Monthly Magazine, December 1901
Medium: Black-and-white oil
Size: 24 x 18 inches
Lender: Brown County Library

30 The Challenge Composition Class Drawing, awarded to N. C. Wyeth by Mr. Pyle on April 7, 1903 Reproduced in *Howard Pyle's Book of Pirates* Harper Brothers, 1921
Medium: India ink
Size: 13 x 7 inches
Lender: Mr. Andrew Wyeth

31 The Forest Madmen Saveth The Life of King Arthur (*The Story of Sir Lancelot and His Companions* by Howard Pyle) Scribners, 1907
Medium: Pen & ink
Size: 10 x 7 inches
Lender: Anonymous

32 Then the Real Fight Began (*Pennsylvania's Defiance of the United States* by H. L. Carson) Harpers Monthly Magazine, October 1908
Medium: Oil on canvas
Size: 30⅛ x 21½ inches
Lender: Mr. and Mrs. William Sipple

33   Decorative Title Page and Initial "T" (*The Salem Wolf* by Howard Pyle) Harpers Monthly Magazine, December 1909
Medium: Oil on illustration board
Size: 24 x 16 inches
Lender: Anonymous

34   Once It Chased Dr. Wilkinson into The Very Town Itself (*The Salem Wolf* by Howard Pyle) Harpers Monthly Magazine, December 1909
Medium: Oil on canvas
Size: 28 x 18 inches
Lender: Anonymous

35   She Saw Herself for What He Had Said, and Swooned (*The Castle on the Dunes* by Josephine Bacon) Harpers Monthly Magazine, September 1909
Medium: Oil on canvas
Size: 27 x 18 inches
Lender: Anonymous

36   Sir Geraint and The Knight of The Sparrow Hawk
(*The Story of the Grail and the Passing of Arthur* by Howard Pyle) Scribners, 1910
Medium: Pen & ink
Size: 10 x 7 inches
Lender: Anonymous

A·VERSE·WITH·A·MORAL·BUT·NO·NAME·:·

A wise man once, of Haarlem town,
Went wandering up, and wandering down
And ever the question asked:

"If all the world was paper,
    And if all the sea was ink,
And if the trees were bread and cheese,
    What would we do for drink?"

Then all the folk, both great and small,
    Began to beat their brains,
But they could not answer him at all,
    In spite of all their pains.

But still he wandered here and there,
    That man of great renown,
And still he questioned everywhere,
    The folk of Haarlem town:

"If all the world was paper,
    And if all the sea was ink,
And if the trees were bread and cheese,
    What would we do for drink?"

Full thin he grew, as, day by day,
    He toiled with mental strain,
Until the wind blew him away,
    And he ne'er was seen again.

And now methinks I hear you say,
"Was ere a man so foolish, pray,
    Since first the world began?"
Oh, hush! I'll tell you secretly,
Down East there dwells a man, and he
Is asking questions constantly,
That none can answer, that I see;
    Yet he's a wise-wise man!

HOWARD PYLE **2** **"I Am Captain John Mackra" Said I, and Sat Down Upon the Gunwale of the Boat** 1888

HOWARD PYLE **3** **Morgan at Porto Bello** 1888

21

HOWARD PYLE   **7   The Little Maid at The Door**   1892

HOWARD PYLE **8** **The Wreck** 1892

HOWARD PYLE **9 Along The Canal in Old Manhattan** 1893

HOWARD PYLE **12 He Found the Captain Agreeable and Companionable** 1894

HOWARD PYLE   **13   Mr. Parker Stood Looking Steadily at His Visitor**   1895

HOWARD PYLE **16 Through Peaceful Stretches** 1896
HOWARD PYLE **15 Floating Neighbors** 1896

HOWARD PYLE **18** **Nelson Sealing His Letter to The Crown Prince of Denmark** 1897

The Challenge
Studio April 7 1903.
H. Pyle. del.

HOWARD PYLE **19 Burial of Braddock** 1898

HOWARD PYLE   **27   Arrival of Stuyvesant in New Amsterdam**   1901

HOWARD PYLE **35 She Saw Herself for What He Had Said, and Swooned** 1909

Howard Pyle & His Students

37 Endicott Cutting the Cross Out of The English Flag
(Howard Pyle) from *An English Nation* by Thomas
Wentworth Higginson
Harpers New Monthly Magazine, April 1863
Medium: Gouache
Size: 16 x 13⅝ inches
Lender: Anonymous

38 Soldier (Bertha C. Day Bates) circa 1898
Costumed Figure Study
Medium: Oil on canvas
Size: 30 x 20 inches
Lender: Mrs. J. Marshall Cole

39 Soldier (Katherine Pyle) circa 1898
Costumed Figure Study
Medium: Oil on canvas
Size: 30 x 20 inches
Lender: Anonymous

40 Puritan (Frank E. Schoonover) 1898
Medium: Oil on canvas
Size: 25 x 16 inches
Lender: Mr. and Mrs. Douglas Allen

41 Puritan (Unknown Student of Howard Pyle)
Medium: Oil on canvas
Size: 25 x 16 inches
Lender: Mr. and Mrs. Richard V. King

42 Drummer Boy, A Chadds Ford Study
(F.E. Schoonover) 1898
Medium: Oil on canvas
Size: 35½ x 23 inches
Lender: Mr. F.E. Schoonover

43 Canadian Trapper (F.E. Schoonover) from *White
Fang* by Jack London
Outing Magazine, 1906
Medium: Oil on canvas
Size: 36 x 20½ inches
Lender: Mr. and Mrs. Andrew Wyeth

44 The Immigrants (Ellen B. Thompson) from *Janice
Meredith* by Paul Leicester Ford
Dodd, Mead & Company, 1899
Medium: Oil on canvas
Size: 25½ x 17½ inches
Lender: Mr. Chester Marron

45 Chadds Ford Study of Revolutionary Soldier
(Stanley M. Arthurs) 1900
Medium: Oil on canvas
Size: 23 x 16¼ inches
Lender: Mrs. Charles Allmond III

46 Troops Burning Ships at York (Stanley M. Arthurs)
from *The War of 1812* by Captain A. T. Mahan
Scribners Magazine, July 1904
Medium: Oil on canvas
Size: 35 x 23½ inches
Lender: Anonymous

47 Man with A Pistol (N.C. Wyeth) circa 1903
Medium: Oil on canvas
Size: 29 x 22½ inches
Lender: Mrs. A. J. Sordoni

48 Whaling (Clifford Ashley) 1905
Medium: Oil on canvas
Size: 20 x 30 inches
Lender: Mr. and Mrs. George T. Weymouth

49 Across the Rhine (George Harding) 1918
Medium: Watercolor
Size: 8 x 9 inches
Lender: Mr. and Mrs. John Kistler

50 French Villa (George Harding) 1918
Medium: Watercolor
Size: 6¼ x 7½ inches
Lender: Mr. and Mrs. John Kistler

51 Over The Top (Gayle Hoskins) circa 1919
Medium: Oil on canvas
Size: 43 x 36 inches
Lender: Delaware State Armory

52 Strong Medicine (Harvey Dunn) 1935
Medium: Oil on canvas
Size: 30 x 40 inches
Lender: Dr. and Mrs. William A. Morton

HOWARD PYLE **37 Endicott Cutting the Cross Out of The English Flag** 1863

KATHERINE PYLE **39** **Soldier** circa 1898

FRANK E. SCHOONOVER **40** **Puritan** 1898

UNKNOWN STUDENT OF HOWARD PYLE **41** **Puritan**

FRANK E. SCHOONOVER   **42   Drummer Boy, A Chadds Ford Study**   1898
FRANK E. SCHOONOVER   **43   Canadian Trapper**   1906

ELLEN B. THOMPSON **44** **The Immigrants** 1899

STANLEY M. ARTHURS **45** **Chadds Ford Study of Revolutionary Soldier** 1900

CLIFFORD ASHLEY **48 Whaling** 1905

GEORGE HARDING   **49   Across the Rhine**   1918
GEORGE HARDING   **50   French Villa**   1918

N.C. Wyeth

53 Indian Drawings (Eight drawings) 1904
Medium: Pencil
Size: 17¼ x 8½ inches, each
Lender: Mrs. Andrew Wyeth

54 Mowing (Unpublished Illustration) July, 1907
Medium: Oil on canvas
Size: 37½ x 26¾ inches
Lender: Mrs. Andrew Wyeth

55 The Navajo Herder (*Sheepherder of the Southwest* by N. C. Wyeth) Scribner Magazine, January 1909
Medium: Oil on canvas
Size: 37¼ x 28¼ inches
Lender: Mr. and Mrs. Douglas Allen

56 The Sheriff 1909
Medium: Oil on canvas
Size: 25 x 29⅞ inches
Lender: Charles Scribner's Sons

57 Winter (*The Moods* by George T. Marsh) Scribners Magazine, December 1909
Medium: Oil on canvas
Size: 33½ x 30 inches
Lender: Mr. Andrew Wyeth

58 Blind Pew (*Treasure Island* by Robert Louis Stevenson) Scribner's Illustrated Classics, 1911
Medium: Oil on canvas
Size: 50 x 40 inches
Lender: Mrs. Andrew Wyeth

59 At The "Admiral Benbow" (*Treasure Island* by Robert Louis Stevenson) Scribner's Illustrated Classics, 1911
Medium: Oil on canvas
Size: 50 x 40 inches
Lender: Mrs. John W. McCoy II

60 Ben Gunn (*Treasure Island* by Robert Louis Stevenson) Scribner's Illustrated Classics, 1911
Medium: Oil on canvas
Size: 50 x 40 inches
Lender: Mrs. Andrew Wyeth

61 Captain Bill Bones (*Treasure Island* by Robert Louis Stevenson) Scribner's Illustrated Classics, 1911
Medium: Oil on canvas
Size: 50 x 40 inches
Lender: Mrs. Brigham Britton

62 The Hostage (*Treasure Island* by Robert Louis Stevenson) Scribner's Illustrated Classics, 1911
Medium: Oil on canvas
Size: 50 x 40 inches
Lender: Mrs. Brigham Britton

63 In The Galley with Long John Silver (*Treasure Island* by Robert Louis Stevenson) Scribner's Illustrated Classics, 1911
Medium: Oil on canvas
Size: 50 x 40 inches
Lender: Mrs. Andrew Wyeth

64 Jim Hawkins Leaves Home (*Treasure Island* by Robert Louis Stevenson) Scribner's Illustrated Classics, 1911
Medium: Oil on canvas
Size: 50 x 40 inches
Lender: Wilmington Y.M.C.A.

65 Serving Out The Weapons (*Treasure Island* by Robert Louis Stevenson) Scribner's Illustrated Classics, 1911
Medium: Oil on canvas
Size: 50 x 40 inches
Lender: Mr. Andrew Wyeth

66 The Vedette (*The Long Roll* by Mary Johnston) Houghton Mifflin Company, 1911
Medium: Oil on canvas
Size: 50 x 40 inches
Lender: Mr. and Mrs. George A. Weymouth

67 Road to Vidalia (*Cease Firing* by Mary Johnston) Houghton Mifflin Company, 1912
Medium: Oil on canvas
Size: 50 x 40 inches
Lender: Mr. James Wyeth

68 A Dozen Men Crowded In (*Sally Castleton, Southerner* by Crittendon Marriott) Lippincott, 1913
Medium: Oil on canvas
Size: 46 x 37½
Lender: Mr. Leroy Benge, Sr.

69 Fence Builders 1915
Medium: Oil on canvas
Size: 37½ x 49⅓ inches
Lender: Mr. and Mrs. Carl D. Pratt

70 Self-Portrait 1915
Medium: Oil on canvas
Size: 18¼ x 12¼
Lender: Mrs. N. C. Wyeth

71   The Black Arrow Flieth Nevermore (*The Black Arrow* by R. L. Stevenson) Scribner's Illustrated Classics, 1916
Medium: Oil on canvas
Size: 40 x 32 inches
Lender: Mr. Andrew Wyeth

72   Fight on The Plains (*The Great West That Was* by William F. Cody) Hearst's Magazine, 1916
Medium: Oil on canvas
Size: 32 x 40 inches
Lender: Mr. Andrew Wyeth

73   Study for "Newborn Calf" 1917
Medium: Oil on canvas
Size: 25 x 30 inches
Lender: Mr. and Mrs. Daniel W. Dietrich II

74   New Born Calf 1917
Medium: Oil on canvas
Size: 42 x 49 inches
Lender: Mrs. Andrew Wyeth

75   He Blew Three Deadly Notes (*The Boy's King Arthur* by Sidney Lanier) Scribner's Illustrated Classics, 1917
Medium: Oil on canvas
Size: 40 x 32 inches
Lender: Mr. Andrew Wyeth

76   Masquerade (*Last of the Mohicans* by James Fenimore Cooper) Scribner's Illustrated Classics, 1919
Medium: Oil on canvas
Size: 40 x 32 inches
Lender: Brandywine River Museum

77   Still Life (With Dusty Bottle) circa 1920
Medium: Oil on canvas
Size: 37 x 40 inches
Lender: Mrs. William Phelps

78   The Huron Flew Through the Air (*Deerslayer* by J. F. Cooper) Scribners, 1927
Medium: Oil on canvas
Size: 40 x 32 inches
Lender: Mr. and Mrs. Richard Riegel, Jr.

46

N.C. WYETH   **55   The Navajo Herder**   1909

48

N.C. WYETH **57 Winter** 1909

N.C. WYETH **58 Blind Pew** 1911

N.C. WYETH **59 At The "Admiral Benbow"** 1911

N.C. WYETH **60 Ben Gunn** 1911

N.C. WYETH **66** **The Vedette** 1911

N.C. WYETH **67** **Road to Vidalia** 1912

N.C. WYETH **70 Self-Portrait** 1915

N.C. WYETH **72 Fight on The Plains** 1916
N.C. WYETH **73 Study for "Newborn Calf"** 1917

N.C. WYETH   **74   New Born Calf**   1917

N.C. WYETH **78 The Huron Flew Through the Air** 1927

Andrew Wyeth

79 Young Buck 1945
Medium: Watercolor
Size: 29 x 22¾ inches
Lender: Mr. and Mrs. Glascow Reynolds

80 The Children's Doctor 1949
Medium: Tempera
Size: 26 x 25 inches
Lender: Dr. Margaret I. Handy

81 Trodden Weed 1951
Medium: Tempera
Size: 20 x 18¼ inches
Lender: Mrs. Andrew Wyeth

82 Faraway 1952
Medium: Dry brush
Size: 13½ x 21 inches
Lender: Mrs. Andrew Wyeth

83 Flock of Crows 1953
Medium: Dry brush
Size: 9½ x 19 inches
Lender: Mrs. Andrew Wyeth

84 James Loper 1953
Medium: Tempera
Size: 48 x 30 inches
Lender: Brandywine River Museum

85 Nicholas 1955
Medium: Tempera
Size: 32½ x 30¾ inches
Lender: Mrs. Andrew Wyeth

86 Quaker Ladies 1956
Medium: Dry brush
Size: 13¾ x 22 inches
Lender: Anonymous

87 Roasted Chestnuts 1956
Medium: Tempera
Size: 48 x 33 inches
Lender: Brandywine River Museum

88 Snow Flurries 1956
Medium: Tempera
Size: 36 x 47 inches
Lender: Dr. Margaret I. Handy

89 The Mill 1958
Medium: Dry brush
Size: 12 x 22¼ inches
Lender: Mrs. Andrew Wyeth

90 Raccoon 1958
Medium: Tempera
Size: 48 x 48 inches
Lender: The Honorable and Mrs. Harry G. Haskell, Jr.

91 Fungus 1959
Medium: Watercolor
Size: 29¾ x 21½ inches
Lender: Mr. and Mrs. J. Bruce Bredin

92 May Day 1960
Medium: Watercolor
Size: 12¾ x 29 inches
Lender: Mrs. Andrew Wyeth

93 Young Bull 1960
Medium: Dry brush
Size: 20⅛ x 41⅝ inches
Lender: Mrs. Andrew Wyeth

94 Above Archie's 1961
Medium: Watercolor drawing
Size: 16½ x 28 inches
Lender: Mrs. Andrew Wyeth

95 The Granary 1961
Medium: Watercolor
Size: 13⅝ x 21⅝ inches
Lender: Mrs. Andrew Wyeth

96 Milk Cans 1961
Medium: Dry brush drawing
Size: 13¼ x 20¾ inches
Lender: Mrs. Andrew Wyeth

97 British at Brandywine 1962
Medium: Dry brush
Size: 19½ x 25½
Lender: Mr. and Mrs. Walter J. Laird, Jr.

98 Garrett Room 1962
Medium: Dry brush
Size: 17½ x 22½ inches
Lender: Mrs. Andrew Wyeth

99 Fur Hat 1963
Medium: Pencil with watercolor
Size: 15¾ x 23¼ inches
Lender: Mrs. Andrew Wyeth

100 Marsh Hawk 1964
Medium: Tempera
Size: 30½ x 45 inches
Lender: Dr. Margaret I. Handy

101 The Drifter 1964
Medium: Dry brush
Size: 22½ x 28½ inches
Lender: Mrs. Andrew Wyeth

102 Chain Hoist 1965
Medium: Watercolor
Size: 20 x 28 inches
Lender: Anonymous

103 Maga's Daughter 1966
Medium: Tempera
Size: 26½ x 30¼ inches
Lender: Mr. Andrew Wyeth

104 River Valley 1966
Medium: Watercolor
Size: 21¾ x 30 inches
Lender: Mrs. Andrew Wyeth

105 French Twist 1967
Medium: Dry brush
Size: 22½ x 28½ inches
Lender: Mrs. Andrew Wyeth

106 Slight Breeze 1968
Medium: Tempera
Size: 24½ x 32½ inches
Lender: Mr. and Mrs. James Wyeth

107 Willard's Coat 1968
Medium: Dry brush
Size: 29½ x 21 inches
Lender: Mr. Nicholas Wyeth

108 Grackles in the Trees 1969
Medium: Watercolor
Size: 22 x 30 inches
Lender: Mr. and Mrs. Carl A. Cantera

109 Dam Breast 1970
Medium: Watercolor
Size: 20½ x 29⅜ inches
Lender: Mr. Andrew Wyeth

110 Evening At Kuerner's 1970
Medium: Dry brush
Size: 25½ x 39¾ inches
Lender: Mrs. Andrew Wyeth

111 Lynch 1970
Medium: Dry brush
Size: 21 x 29 inches
Lender: Mr. and Mrs. John W. Rollins, Jr.

112 New Coat 1970
Medium: Watercolor
Size: 13½ x 18½ inches
Lender: Mrs. Dorothy Theodore

113 Siri 1970
Medium: Tempera
Size: 30 x 30½ inches
Lender: Mr. Andrew Wyeth

114 Spruce Grove 1970
Medium: Watercolor
Size: 18½ x 27½ inches
Lender: Chadds Ford Gallery

115 Under Cover 1970
Medium: Dry brush
Size: 27 x 39 inches
Lender: Mr. Andrew Wyeth

116 Watch Dog 1970
Medium: Watercolor
Size: 28½ x 22½ inches
Lender: Mr. and Mrs. Norman L. Cahners

117 Anna Kuerner 1971
Medium: Tempera
Size: 13½ x 19¼ inches
Lender: Mr. Andrew Wyeth

118 The Kuerners 1971
Medium: Dry brush
Size: 25 x 40 inches
Lender: Mr. Andrew Wyeth

119 Ice Storm 1971
Medium: Dry brush
Size: 28¼ x 22¼ inches
Lender: Mr. Frederick C. Church

ANDREW WYETH **119 Ice Storm** 1971

ANDREW WYETH   **79   Young Buck**   1945

ANDREW WYETH **81 Trodden Weed** 1951

ANDREW WYETH **82 Faraway** 1952

ANDREW WYETH **84 James Loper** 1953

ANDREW WYETH **85 Nicholas** 1955

ANDREW WYETH **86 Quaker Ladies** 1956

ANDREW WYETH **113** **Siri** 1970

ANDREW WYETH **87 Roasted Chestnuts** 1956

ANDREW WYETH **88 Snow Flurries** 1956

ANDREW WYETH **89 The Mill** 1958

ANDREW WYETH **93 Young Bull** 1960

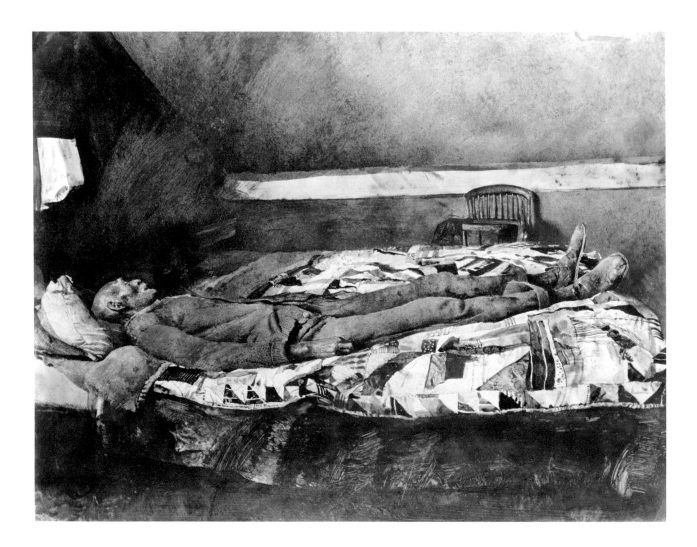

ANDREW WYETH **98 Garrett Room** 1962

ANDREW WYETH   **114   Spruce Grove**   1970

ANDREW WYETH **100 Marsh Hawk** 1964

ANDREW WYETH **102** **Chain Hoist** 1965

ANDREW WYETH **117 Anna Kuerner** 1971

ANDREW WYETH **104** **River Valley** 1966

84

ANDREW WYETH **108 Grackles in the Trees** 1969

85

ANDREW WYETH **110 Evening at Kuerner's** 1970

ANDREW WYETH **115 Under Cover** 1970

ANDREW WYETH **116 Watch Dog** 1970

ANDREW WYETH **112** **New Coat** 1970

James Wyeth

120 Lester 1963
Medium: Oil on canvas
Size: 26 x 20 inches
Lender: Mr. and Mrs. George E. Kearns, Jr.

121 Mushroom Picker 1963
Medium: Oil on canvas
Size: 30 x 49 inches
Mr. and Mrs. H.T. Hilliard

122 Shorty 1963
Medium: Oil on canvas
Size: 18½ x 22½ inches
Lender: Mrs. Andrew Wyeth

123 The Record Player 1964
Medium: Oil on canvas
Size: 47 x 28 inches
Lender: Mr. and Mrs. Edwin E. Tullis

124 Below the Barn 1965
Medium: Watercolor
Size: 19 x 28 inches
Lender: Anonymous

125 Draft Age 1965
Medium: Oil on canvas
Size: 36 x 30 inches
Lender: Mr. Jeffrey Theodore

126 Root Cellar 1966
Medium: Watercolor
Size: 28 x 19 inches
Lender: Amanda K. Berls

127 Portrait of Jeffrey 1966
Medium: Oil on canvas
Size: 19 x 20 inches
Lender: Mrs. James Theodore

128 Portrait of Governor Charles L. Terry, Jr. 1966
Medium: Oil on canvas
Size: 23 x 27 inches
Lender: The State of Delaware

129 Portrait of President John F. Kennedy 1967
Medium: Oil on canvas
Size: 16 x 29 inches
Lender: Anonymous

**Preliminary Studies (1966-1967) for
Portrait of President John F. Kennedy**

130 President John F. Kennedy
Medium: Oil on gesso
Size: 15½ x 19¾ inches
Lender: Mr. and Mrs. James Wyeth

131 President John F. Kennedy
Full-Scale Preparatory Study
Medium: Pencil
Size: 16¼ x 27½ inches
Lender: Mr. and Mrs. James Wyeth

132 President John F. Kennedy
(Walking, Hands in Pocket)
Medium: Pencil
Size: 14¼ x 16¼ inches
Lender: Mr. and Mrs. James Wyeth

133 President John F. Kennedy
Medium: Pencil
Size: 13½ x 15½ inches
Lender: Mr. and Mrs. James Wyeth

134 President John F. Kennedy
Medium: Pencil
Size: 14 x 11 inches
Lender: Mr. Frederick L. Holborn

135 Senator Edward M. Kennedy
Medium: Pencil
Size: 14 x 11½ inches
Lender: Mr. and Mrs. James Wyeth

**136 Senator Robert F. Kennedy
Senator Edward M. Kennedy**
Medium: Pencil
Size: 11 x 14 inches
Lender: Mr. and Mrs. James Wyeth

137 Bronze Age 1967
Medium: Oil on canvas
Size: 24 x 36 inches
Lender: William A. Farnsworth Library and Art Museum

138 Duck, Fence & Stump 1967
Medium: Watercolor
Size: 27½ x 18½ inches
Lender: Anonymous

139 Fog Station 1967
Medium: Watercolor
Size: 19½ x 24½ inches
Lender: Ruth A. Yerion

JAMES WYETH **156 Portrait of Andrew Wyeth** 1969

140 Lattice Work 1967
Medium: Oil on canvas
Size: 15¾ x 11¾ inches
Lender: Mr. and Mrs. Reed Coleman

141 Bailing Twine 1968
Medium: Watercolor
Size: 19½ x 24½ inches
Lender: Mr. and Mrs. P.W. Tate Brown

142 Hecking House 1968
Medium: Watercolor
Size: 18½ x 27½ inches
Lender: Mrs. Andrew Wyeth

143 Island Roses 1968
Medium: Watercolor
Size: 19⅜ x 24⅜ inches
Lender: Mrs. Andrew Wyeth

144 Lifeline 1968
Medium: Watercolor
Size: 32 x 27 inches
Lender: Dr. Margaret I. Handy

145 Portrait of George Tener 1968
Medium: Oil on canvas
Size: 37 x 32 inches
Lender: Mr. George E. Tener

146 Ring Bolt 1968
Medium: Watercolor
Size: 19 x 28 inches
Lender: Mr. Robert F. Woolworth

147 River Trunk 1968
Medium: Watercolor
Size: 24 x 17 inches
Lender: Mr. and Mrs. James Wyeth

148 The Tin Woodsman 1968
Medium: Watercolor
Size: 24 x 19 inches
Lender: Mrs. Baird C. Brittingham

149 The Wreck 1968
Medium: Oil on canvas
Size: 20 x 40 inches
Lender: Anonymous

150 Buzz Saw 1969
Medium: Oil on canvas
Size: 30 x 30 inches
Lender: Mr. Richard Levine

151 Island Church 1969
Medium: Watercolor
Size: 19½ x 24½ inches
Lender: Mr. Gordon Hanes

152 Island Burial 1969
Medium: Watercolor
Size: 19 x 30 inches
Lender: Mrs. Charles Seaverns

153 Median Strip 1969
Medium: Oil on canvas
Size: 18½ x 24½ inches
Lender: Mrs. Anne Trecartin

154 Moon Landing 1969
Medium: Oil on canvas
Size: 29 x 43⅛ inches
Lender: Amanda K. Berls

155 Partridge House 1969
Medium: Watercolor
Size: 30 x 19 inches
Lender: Mr. Edward McLaughlin

156 Portrait of Andrew Wyeth 1969
Medium: Oil on canvas
Size: 24 x 32 inches
Lender: Mr. and Mrs. James Wyeth

157 Pot 1969
Medium: Oil on canvas
Size: 18 x 24 inches
Lender: Mr. and Mrs. James Wyeth

158 Spring Plowing 1969
Medium: Watercolor
Size: 19¾ x 30 inches
Lender: Dr. Norman Crisp

159 Twin Houses 1969
Medium: Watercolor
Size: 19 x 29¾ inches
Lender: Mr. Alexander F. Treadwell

160 The Wreck of the D.T. Sheridan 1969
Medium: Watercolor
Size: 19 x 30 inches
Lender: Mr. David Hilyard

161 Cooling Off 1970
Medium: Watercolor
Size: 22 x 30 inches
Lender: Mr. J. Robinson West

162 Gull Rock 1970
Medium: Oil on canvas
Size: 25 x 40⅛ inches
Lender: Mr. J. Robinson West

163 John Cabot III 1970
Medium: Watercolor
Size: 16 x 19 inches
Lender: Mr. Nicholas Wyeth

164 Overgrowth 1970
Medium: Watercolor
Size: 22 x 30 inches
Lender: Mr. and Mrs. James P. Mills

165 Pig 1970
Medium: Oil on canvas
Size: 4 feet x 7 feet
Lender: Mrs. Andrew Wyeth

166 Pig House 1970
Medium: Watercolor
Size: 30½ x 21¾ inches
Lender: Mr. and Mrs. James Wyeth

167 Sea of Storms 1970
Medium: Oil on canvas
Size: 38½ x 45 inches
Lender: Mr. and Mrs. James Wyeth

168 Squid 1970
Medium: Watercolor
Size: 18½ x 29½ inches
Lender: Chadds Ford Gallery

169 Trap 1970
Medium: Watercolor
Size: 30 x 21 inches
Lender: Mr. Eugene Dixon

170 Zero 1970
Medium: Watercolor
Size: 19 x 30 inches
Lender: Mr. Brownlee O. Curry

JAMES WYETH **126 Root Cellar** 1966

JAMES WYETH **121 Mushroom Picker** 1963

JAMES WYETH **125** **Draft Age** 1965

JAMES WYETH   **133**   **President John F. Kennedy**   1966-1967

JAMES WYETH   **136**   **Senator Robert F. Kennedy and Edward M. Kennedy**   1966–1967

FRECKLES ON FOREHEAD
PINKY BROWN

JAMES WYETH **135 Senator Edward M. Kennedy** 1966–1967

JAMES WYETH   **129   Portrait of President John F. Kennedy**   1967

JAMES WYETH **137 Bronze Age** 1967

JAMES WYETH **140 Lattice Work** 1967

JAMES WYETH **139** **Fog Station** 1967

JAMES WYETH **147 River Trunk** 1968

106

JAMES WYETH **150 Buzz Saw** 1969

JAMES WYETH **162 Gull Rock** 1970

JAMES WYETH **154** **Moon Landing** 1969

JAMES WYETH **157** **Pot** 1969

JAMES WYETH **165** **Pig** 1970

JAMES WYETH **158 Spring Plowing** 1969

JAMES WYETH **161 Cooling Off** 1970

JAMES WYETH **163** **John Cabot III** 1970

JAMES WYETH **166 Pig House** 1970

JAMES WYETH **167 Sea of Storms** 1970

JAMES WYETH **168 Squid** 1970

JAMES WYETH **169 Trap** 1970